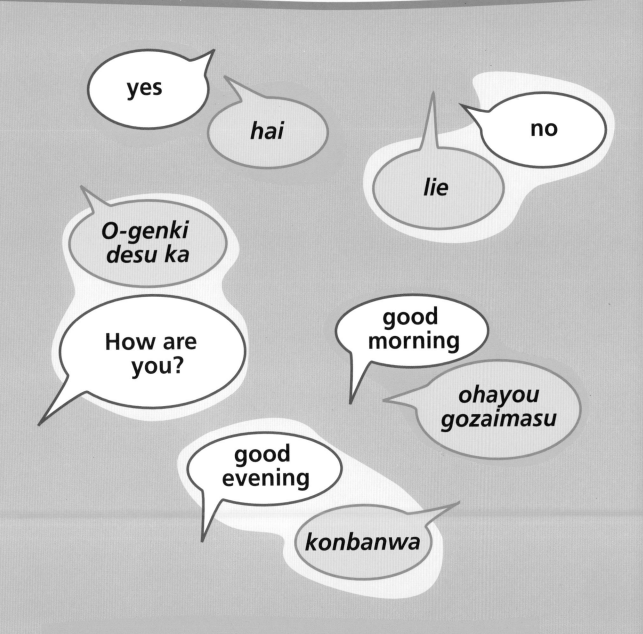

English words that come from Japanese

samurai dojo kimono

haiku

tsunami karate tofu Zen

Welcome to Japan

Meredith Costain   Paul Collins

This edition first published in 2002 in the United States of America by Chelsea House Publishers, a subsidiary of Haights Cross Communications

Chelsea House Publishers
1974 Sproul Road, Suite 400
Broomall, PA 19008–0914

The Chelsea House world wide web address is www.chelseahouse.com

Library of Congress Cataloging-in-Publication Data Applied for.
ISBN 0-7910-6541-3

First published in 2000 by
Macmillan Education Australia Pty Ltd
627 Chapel Street, South Yarra, Australia, 3141

Copyright © Meredith Costain and Paul Collins 2000

Edited by Miriana Dasovic
Text design by Goanna Graphics (Vic) Pty Ltd
Page layout by Goanna Graphics (Vic) Pty Ltd
Cover design by Goanna Graphics (Vic) Pty Ltd
Printed in Hong Kong

Acknowledgements

The author and the publisher are grateful to the following for permission to reproduce copyright material:

Cover photograph: Children dress up for Children's Day Festival, Great Southern Stock/© Alan Elliot.

Great Southern Stock, pp. 5, 7 (bottom), 8, 10, 11 (top & bottom) & p. 12 © Alan Elliot, p. 13 (bottom) © Richard I'Anson, p. 14 © Alan Elliot, p. 15 (top) © AFE, pp. 15 (bottom) & 18 © Alan Elliot, p. 19 (top) © Richard I'Anson, pp. 19 (bottom) & 20 © Alan Elliot, p. 21 (top) © Richard I'Anson, p. 23 (top) © Alan Elliot, p. 23 (bottom) © Jim Hooper, pp. 25 (top), 26, 28 & 29 (top) © Alan Elliot; Japanese Information Service, pp. 9 (top), 21 (bottom), 22, 24, 29 (bottom), 30; Gillian Jones, pp. 13 (top), 15 (middle), 27 (bottom); Lonely Planet Images, p. 9 (bottom) © Richard I'Anson, p. 25 (bottom) © Frank Carter, p. 27 (top) © Di Mayfield; Kiyoshi Miyazawa, pp. 6, 7 (top); PhotoDisc, p 30.

While every care has been taken to trace and acknowledge copyright the publishers tender their apologies for any accidental infringement where copyright has proved untraceable.

Contents

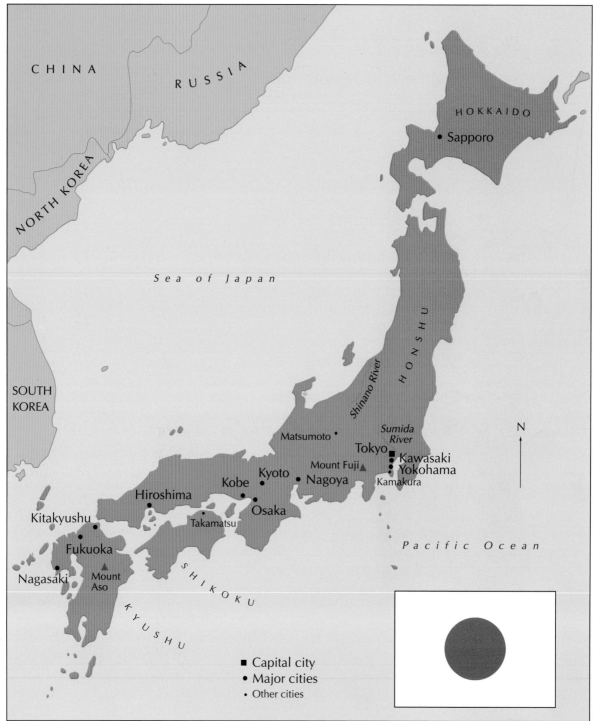

CHINA

RUSSIA

NORTH KOREA

HOKKAIDO

• Sapporo

Sea of Japan

SOUTH KOREA

HONSHU

Shinano River

Matsumoto •

Sumida River

Tokyo ■

Kawasaki

Yokohama

Kamakura

Mount Fuji ▲

Kyoto

Nagoya

Kobe

Hiroshima

Osaka

Kitakyushu

Takamatsu •

Fukuoka

SHIKOKU

Nagasaki

Mount Aso ▲

KYUSHU

Pacific Ocean

N

■ Capital city
• Major cities
• Other cities

Welcome to Japan!

Konnichiwa! My name is Mitsuko. I live in Matsumoto, which is a small city in the **prefecture** of Nagano, in Japan.

Japan is a long narrow country, made up of nearly 4,000 islands. The four biggest islands are Hokkaido, Honshu, Kyushu and Shikoku. Matsumoto is on Honshu, about 150 kilometers (93 miles) northwest of the capital Tokyo. Honshu, the largest of all the islands, is known as the 'mainland' of Japan.

Our nearest neighbors are Russia, Korea and China. Our flag is called *hinomaru,* which means 'circle of the sun'. Our emperors claim to be descended from Amaterasu O-mikami, the Sun Goddess. We call our country *Nihon* or Nippon, which means 'source of the sun'.

Japan is one of the most densely populated countries in the world. More than two-thirds of our land area is covered by mountains, and three-quarters of our population live in cities.

Today I am wearing my best **kimono** *for the Seven-Five-Three Festival. Normally I wear Western clothes.*

Family life

Because a large part of Japan is covered by mountains, there is not much land for buildings. Most houses are small. Many Japanese people live in high-rise apartment buildings called *danchi,* located on the edges of cities.

We always take our shoes off when we are inside the house. The furniture in our house is mainly Western style. However, many homes still have traditional Japanese furniture. My Uncle Akira lives in a suburb of Tokyo. His house has thick mats on the floor, called **tatami**. At night, his family uses them as mattresses to sleep on. There are also sliding doors instead of inside walls. These can be taken out to make the rooms larger.

Like most houses in Japan, our home is built of wood. It is larger than many of the homes in the big cities. My brother Shinya and I are lucky. We each have our own bedroom. We love playing computer games, such as Pokemon *and* Pikatyuu. *We also have two pet hamsters.*

Most Japanese people stay in the same job their whole lives. My father, Yoshiitirou, works very hard in a bank in Matsumoto. He even goes to work when it is a holiday! My mother, Keiko, once worked in the same bank. Now she stays home to look after Shinya and me.

The furniture in our house is Western style.

Traditional Japanese tables have very short legs. People sit or kneel on the floor to eat their meals.

School

Children in Japan start school at the age of six, but many first go to kindergarten for two or three years. We spend six years at elementary school, where we study subjects such as mathematics, Japanese, science, sociology, gymnastics and music. I like gymnastics best! School starts at 8:20 a.m. and finishes at 4:00 p.m. during the week, and we also go to school on Saturday mornings.

After elementary school we spend three years at middle school, then another three years at high school. Many students then go on to study for another four years at university.

To make sure they get into the best high schools and universities, Japanese students study very hard. I always have lots of homework. Some students at junior high also attend *juku*, an 'after-school' school. The final year of high school is called the year of *shiken jigoku* or 'exam hell'.

We always show great respect for our teachers, whom we call **sensei**. This means 'first born'. We begin and end our classes by bowing to our teachers. We also help to keep our school buildings and grounds clean.

All Japanese children wear uniforms to school.

Sports and leisure

Japanese people love sports. Baseball, which we call *yakyu*, is the most popular sport for boys. The major baseball leagues are Pacific and Central. We all play baseball at school, and follow the teams on television.

Other Western sports such as golf, tennis, volleyball and soccer are also popular. In winter, many people visit the Japanese Alps for skiing and other winter sports. In summer, we enjoy sailing, wind-surfing, hiking and fishing.

Many school children belong to clubs. They enjoy listening to music, playing computer games and pinball, and reading comic books called *manga*.

Many Japanese perform martial arts, which have been part of our culture for centuries. Martial arts such as judo, karate and kendo were first practiced by **samurai** *warriors as a way of keeping fit in times of peace.*

Sumo wrestlers eat special food to make themselves as large as possible. Many wrestlers weigh more than 130 kilograms (287 pounds)! They bow, squat and stamp the ground, then try to push each other out of the ring.

Japanese culture

Although the Japanese are big fans of Western culture, we have an ancient and highly developed culture of our own. *Noh,* the oldest form of Japanese drama, grew out of religious dances and rituals from the 1200s. All the characters, including the female ones, are played by male actors, wearing masks and beautiful costumes. The plays tell ancient stories of ghosts, demons, gods and warriors.

The heroes in *kabuki* theater are often samurai warriors and, once again, all the parts are played by men. There are lots of special tricks in *kabuki,* such as revolving stages and trap-doors. In *bunraku,* the characters are played by puppets which are half the size of real people. The puppeteers are so skilled that the puppets seem to be alive!

Drama performances are often accompanied by music played on traditional Japanese instruments. These include a bamboo flute called the *shakuhachi,* a 3-string instrument called the *shamisen,* a 13-string instrument called the *koto,* and a drum known as the *taiko.*

Japanese theater involves music and dance.

Haiku, the art of writing a poem using three lines and 17 syllables, was developed by a Japanese poet named Basho in the 1600s. The poems tell of the glories of nature: mountains, the sun and the moon, the seasons, and our beautiful cherry blossom.

Behold the green frog	[5 syllables]
Hopping through the lily pond	[7 syllables]
His long tongue flicking	[5 syllables]

An example of haiku.

The Tea Ceremony has been performed since the 1400s. It is held in a specially built tea house in a traditional garden, and lasts for up to four hours. Guests eat a sweet, sip their tea and then admire the beauty of the cup. The calm surroundings help people to forget about their problems.

Many Japanese people take lessons in ikebana, *the art of flower arranging. Flowers are placed in specially shaped containers according to strict rules. Many people also grow miniature trees, called* bonsai. *The trees are pruned and wired into different shapes.*

Festivals and religion

We have many festivals and national holidays in Japan. Our most important holiday is *Oshogatsu*, New Year's Holiday. All the shops, offices and factories close for three days so that we can meet up with our families and friends. On New Year's Eve, we dress up in our best kimonos and go to our local temple or shrine to pray for health and happiness in the coming year. The next day we exchange gifts and cards. We eat special holiday food such as pounded rice cakes, rice cake stew, fish roe and seaweed. It's delicious! In summer we hold the *Obon* Festival, to honor the dead.

My favorite festival is Children's Day, held in May. All the boys tie huge paper streamers, shaped like **carp**, to poles in the garden and on the roofs of their houses. There is a special festival in March for girls. They display beautiful dolls dressed in kimonos in their homes. In November, girls aged seven, boys aged five, and all three-year-olds are taken to local shrines by their parents to offer thanks and prayers for past and future health and luck. This is called the Seven-Five-Three Festival.

Japanese Festivals

New Year	January 1–3
Girls' Festival	March 3
Flower Festival	April 8
Rice-planting Festival	April/May
Children's Day Festival	May 5
Star Festival	July 7
Feast of Lights	July 13–16
Festival of the Dead	August 13–16
Seven-Five-Three	November 15

Children dress up in their best clothes for Children's Day Festival.

There are two main religions in Japan, Shinto and Buddhism. However, most people follow parts of both religions in their daily lives. Many people are baptized and married in Shinto shrines, but buried in Buddhist temples, because they believe that Buddha looks after the dying and the dead.

Shinto is the oldest religion, dating back to the time of ancient folk myths and beliefs. It is only found in Japan, and means 'the way of the gods'. Followers of Shinto believe that all natural things contain spiritual forces, or gods, called **kami**. Shrines and temples, built to give thanks and to pray to the gods, are found all over Japan.

A gateway, or **torii**, *marks the entrance to a Shinto shrine.*

Buddhism developed in India and was brought to Japan from China in around AD 500. Buddhists believe that you can find the true meaning of life by living simply. Many Japanese families have shrines in their home where they pay their respects to their ancestors.

Worshippers pay their respects at Asakasa Shrine in Tokyo.

Food and shopping

Traditional Japanese food is very different from Western food. Our diet is very healthy. Most of our meals are based around rice, fish and vegetables. The fish can be fried, steamed or grilled, and is often eaten raw! We usually eat with chopsticks instead of knives and forks. Green tea is served with every meal.

My favorite fish dish is *sushi*. Thin slices of fish are served on top of small blocks of rice that have been cooked in rice wine and vinegar. I also like *sashimi*, which is raw fish served with soy sauce, ginger and fiery horseradish. Other foods we eat include dried seaweed called *nori*, vegetables and seafood in batter called *tempura*, miso soup made from soya beans, and *sukiyaki*, a dish of sliced meat and vegetables cooked in soy sauce.

My father takes a little lunch box, called a *bento*, to work every day. It contains rice, vegetables, meat, raw fish and pickles. Japanese people love Western-style take-out food, too. There are lots of fast-food and drive-in restaurants selling pizza, hamburgers and fried chicken.

Japanese cooks take great care when preparing and presenting food. Even the bowls the food is served in are chosen for their color and shape.

Tokyo is a shopping paradise! Its most famous shopping street is the Ginza. There are huge department stores crammed with everything you could want to buy, from food to computer games. Many shopping centers are built around busy railway stations. The stores stay open until very late. You can even buy new shoes or a comic book at midnight if you want to.

Japanese people love toys, electronic games and knick-knacks. There are stalls all over the cities selling games, toys, kites, masks, and sports equipment.

Many people shop at outdoor markets and food stalls.

Make tempura

Tempura is a popular Japanese dish. Small pieces of fish, shrimp and vegetables are fried quickly in a light batter. You need to eat *tempura* as soon as it is cooked, while it is crisp and crunchy.

Ask an adult to help you prepare this dish.

What you need:

- 1 small fish fillet
- shrimp, cleaned and deveined
- vegetables – choose from potato, sweet potato, pumpkin, green beans, red or green peppers, cauliflower, or eggplant
- 2 eggs
- 1 cup cold water
- 3/4 cup sifted plain flour
- oil for deep frying
- soy sauce
- paper towels for drainage

What to do:

1 Slice the vegetables into thin strips.

2 Make the batter by beating the eggs, then add the water and flour all at once. Blend thoroughly.

3 Heat the oil in a deep pan or wok until it is very hot.

4 Using tongs to hold them, dip the vegetables and seafood into the batter. Quickly deep-fry them, a few at a time, turning once or twice until they are crisp.

5 Using a slotted spoon, take the *tempura* out of the pan and drain the oil from them on paper towels.

6 Place the *tempura* in small china bowls.

7 Using chopsticks, dip the *tempura* in soy sauce and eat straightaway!

Make a *ningyo* doll

These *ningyo* dolls, dressed in traditional kimonos, have magic in them!

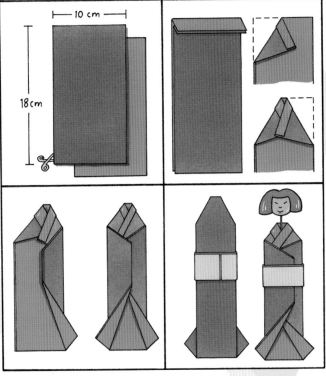

You will need:

- 4 pieces of colored paper, each one a different color
- scissors
- felt-tip pens
- glue
- a toothpick

What to do:

1 Choose two pieces of paper. On each piece, cut out a rectangle 10 cm by 18 cm (4 in by 7 in).

2 Put the rectangles on top of each other. Fold a little bit of the top edge over.

3 Turn the rectangles over. The folded edge should be on the underside.

4 Find the middle point of the folded edge. Fold over the left corner.

5 Fold the right corner over the left corner.

6 Fold over the right side of the paper. Fold out the bottom right corner.

7 Do the same with the left side.

8 Cut a strip of paper 2 cm by 11 cm (0.75 in by 4.25 in) from the third piece of colored paper.

9 Wrap it round the middle of the doll, to form a sash for the kimono. Glue one edge over the other.

10 Draw the doll's head on the fourth piece of paper. Draw its hair, nose and mouth. Cut out the head and glue it to the end of a toothpick.

11 Push the toothpick into the top opening of the kimono.

Once you have made your *ningyo* doll, ask your friends to touch it. All the bad spirits in their bodies will go into it! Now ask them to throw the doll into a river, so that it is carried to the sea.

Landscape and climate

Japan has many mountains. They cover more than three-quarters of the land, leaving little room for farming and building. There are also many beautiful lakes and fast-flowing rivers that have formed steep, narrow valleys. In coastal regions you will find gentle, sandy beaches and rugged, rocky cliffs.

Ten percent of the world's active volcanoes are found in Japan. Every now and then they erupt, spewing forth steam, lava and ash. Mount Aso, our largest volcano, last erupted in 1992. It is found on Kyushu, which is famous for its hot springs and mud.

Every year, Japan has hundreds of earthquakes. Most of these are mild, but some are strong enough to cause buildings to sway and things to fall off shelves. In 1923 an earthquake destroyed Tokyo. The city caught fire and 125,000 people were killed. Modern Japanese buildings are now made to withstand earthquakes better.

Our climate ranges from subarctic, which is very cold, to subtropical, which is hot and steamy. In Hokkaido, in the north, the summers are cool and the winters harsh and snowy.

Mountains cover more than three-quarters of the land in Japan.

Terraces are cut into the sides of mountains to provide land for farming.

In Kyushu, in the south, the summers are hot and humid and the winters mild. Temperatures are so varied that, in January, you can find daffodils blooming at one end of Japan, while villages at the other end are buried under three meters (10 feet) of snow!

In the late summer and autumn, the southern coastal areas of Japan are sometimes hit by violent **typhoons**. Winds reach up to 200 kilometers (124 miles) an hour and as much as 300 millimeters (12 inches) of rain can fall in a day. The trees in parks and gardens are supported by poles to stop them being blown away.

This is Lake Takamatsu, one of the many beautiful lakes in Japan.

Plants and animals

The mountain regions of Japan are covered with forests, containing many different kinds of trees. **Evergreen** trees include Japanese cedar, cypress and red pine. In winter, cypress trees carry a blanket of snow. **Deciduous** trees include oak and maple. There are also many flowering trees such as camellia, plum, peach, apple and the famous cherry tree, with its beautiful pink blossom in spring.

We have many different native animals in Japan. These include brown bears, wolves, wild boar, deer, raccoons, foxes and monkeys. Snow monkeys can be found in the far north.

You can read about many of our animals in our folktales. The wily fox bewitches people and causes all sorts of mischief by changing itself into a person or another creature. Crows bring bad luck, but rats are lucky animals.

Japanese children love to chase butterflies and dragonflies, and to catch fireflies on summer evenings. Some people catch crickets and grasshoppers and keep them in small bamboo cages so they can listen to them sing.

Many people travel to the country in autumn to see the leaves of the maple trees turn from green to gold.

Cherry blossoms are a symbol of the arrival of spring. Every year, TV reporters try to predict exactly when the trees in different parts of Japan will blossom. On weekends, the countryside is full of people having picnics beneath the cherry blossoms.

The Japanese crane appears in many traditional folktales as a symbol of long life and faithfulness.

Cities and landmarks

Our capital city is Tokyo. It is very large and crowded, with many traffic jams and skyscrapers. There is so little space that many shopping malls are built underground, and some office towers have as many as 60 stories. The tallest building is Tokyo Tower, in Shiba Park. Although it is a busy city, Tokyo is clean and safe. There is little graffiti, litter or crime.

Kyoto was the capital of Japan for 900 years. When the last **shogun** lost his power in 1868, the capital was moved to Tokyo. Many people visit Kyoto to see the traditional shrines, temples and gardens, and to buy silk and pottery.

Our highest mountain is Mount Fuji. On a clear day, you can see it from over 100 kilometers (62 miles) away. Because of its beauty and size, Mount Fuji is the most sacred of all Shinto religious sites. Mount Fuji is also an active volcano. Luckily for the thousands of people who climb it every year, it has not erupted since 1707!

The emperors of Japan once lived in Kyoto, which was the capital from AD 794 to 1868. The Golden Pavilion was built by a nobleman about 600 years ago.

Many people visit the statue of the Great Buddha, built in 1252. It gazes out over the countryside from Kamakura, southwest of Tokyo.

Industry and agriculture

Until 100 years ago, most people in Japan worked on farms. Today, Japan is a highly **industrialized** nation. We lead the world in making cars, electronics, steel, cameras, watches, computers, chemicals, plastics and many other products. A third of our people work in manufacturing industries.

Japan has very few natural resources of its own. We must import large amounts of raw materials such as iron ore, copper, bauxite, cotton and wool, wheat and petroleum. To pay for these imports, we sell many of our goods overseas.

Japan is also a world leader in 'high-tech' industries such as electronics, space research and energy. Huge amounts of money are spent every year on research and development.

Robots are used on many production lines, increasing efficiency and safety. They do many of the dull, dirty and dangerous jobs in factories.

Farming

Some farmers raise pigs, cattle and chickens, or grow fruit and vegetables such as apples, pears, mandarins, tomatoes, potatoes, and cucumbers. Others grow flowers in greenhouses.

Fishing is another important industry. We eat fish every day and catch more fish than any other nation in the world. Our seas are filled with many different kinds of fish including tuna, cod, sardines, shrimp and octopus.

Instead of catching them in the ocean, many people raise fish on fish farms. Saltwater fish such as seabream are kept in sheltered bays, while freshwater fish such as carp and trout are kept in large ponds. Other farmers grow seaweed, such as *nori* and kelp, that is good to eat.

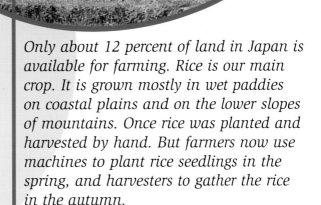

Only about 12 percent of land in Japan is available for farming. Rice is our main crop. It is grown mostly in wet paddies on coastal plains and on the lower slopes of mountains. Once rice was planted and harvested by hand. But farmers now use machines to plant rice seedlings in the spring, and harvesters to gather the rice in the autumn.

Fishing is an important industry in Japan. It is also an important part our daily diet, as we eat more of it than red meat.

Transportation

Public transportation in Japan is fast and reliable. Millions of people in urban areas use trains to get to work. The trains at rush hour fill up so quickly that some stations hire staff to push passengers into the train cabins.

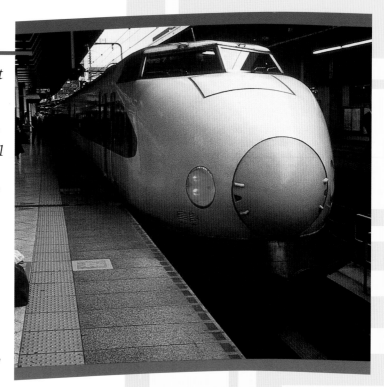

Japan's famous bullet trains are called shinkansen. *They travel at speeds of up to 275 kilometers (171 miles) per hour. It takes only two-and-a-half hours to travel from Tokyo to Osaka, a distance of 550 kilometers (342 miles). Bullet trains always leave and arrive on time. They are so punctual, you can set your watch by them!*

Japanese engineers are working on a new linear motor rail system. These Maglev trains will use magnets to 'float' over tracks at more than 500 kilometers (310 miles) per hour.

About two-thirds of Japanese families own cars. The national road system has been upgraded to handle the huge volumes of traffic between cities. There is so little land for parking in Tokyo, that car owners must prove they have a parking space before they can register their car.

The four main islands are joined by a series of tunnels and bridges. The Seikan Tunnel between Honshu and Hokkaido is 43 kilometers (26.7 miles) long, making it the second-longest tunnel in the world. Some bridges have two levels, one for cars and the other for trains.

Japan has over 1,000 busy ports along its coastline. Lots of cargo ships carry oil, coal, iron ore and manufactured goods in and out of the country. Ferries move people between the smaller and larger islands. You can also travel between most of the major Japanese cities on planes.

Many people living in cities leave their cars at home and use trains to get to work. Commuter trains at rush hour are always packed with passengers.

People living on Japan's small islands depend on boats to get around.

History and government

People have lived on the islands of Japan for thousands of years. In 300 BC, Japan was made up of many small clans, all fighting for power. One strong leader called Yamato took control around AD 400. The emperors who ruled Japan after that were his **descendants**. Life under the emperors was peaceful. They built many fine capital cities, temples and palaces. Over time, however, the emperors became weak and power fell once again into the hands of warrior leaders.

In 1192, a man called Minamoto Yoritomo set up a military government. Military leaders called shoguns became the real rulers of Japan. Every district had a private army of Japanese samurai. Finally, in the late 1500s, three great leaders united Japan into one nation. Japan remained cut off from the rest of the world for the next 200 years. Then Commodore Perry arrived with four American ships in 1853, demanding supplies and the right to trade with Japan.

The samurai warriors lived in castles like this one, which is Hikone Castle. Their buildings were like fortresses, with barred windows and gates. They fired guns and arrows from the small windows. The samurai were fearless. They would kill themselves rather than surrender to the enemy in battle.

Japan then realized it needed to become a modern nation. An **industrial revolution** took place as many people left their farms to work in factories. The samurai were disbanded and the armed forces were used to build up an empire. Japan lost that empire when it was defeated in World War 2. Since then, Japan has made friends with former enemies and has worked hard to rebuild its economy. Other countries now try to copy Japan's success.

In August each year, children make paper cranes and leave them at shrines in Hiroshima and Nagasaki, in memory of the people who died in the atomic bombings that ended World War 2.

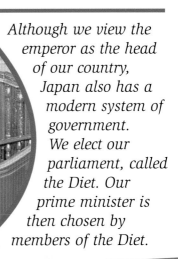

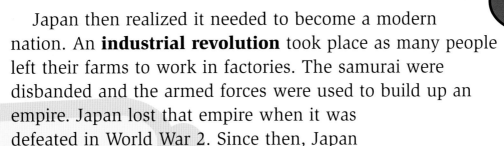

Although we view the emperor as the head of our country, Japan also has a modern system of government. We elect our parliament, called the Diet. Our prime minister is then chosen by members of the Diet.

Fact file

Official name Nippon		**Population** 126,200,000	**Land area** 377,765 square kilometers (147,328 square miles)
Government a democratic government headed by a prime minister	**Language** Japanese		**Religions** Shinto, Buddhism, Christianity
Currency Yen (¥)		**Capital city** Tokyo	**Major cities** Yokohama, Osaka, Nagoya, Sapporo, Kobe, Kyoto, Fukuoka, Kawasaki, Kitakyushu, Hiroshima
Number of islands nearly 4,000	**Main islands** Honshu, Hokkaido, Shikoku, Kyushu	**Climate** varies from hot and humid in the south, to bitterly cold in the north (depending on the season)	
Major rivers Shinano, Sumida			**Highest mountain** Mount Fuji on the island of Honshu 3,776 meters (12,390 feet)
Main farm products rice, vegetables, fruit, cows, pigs, poultry, fish, silk	**Main industries** machinery and equipment, metals and metal products, textiles, cars, chemicals, electrical and electronic equipment		**Natural resources** small amounts of iron ore, coal and oil (most raw materials for industry are imported)

Glossary

carp	a type of freshwater fish
deciduous	plants and trees that lose their leaves in winter
descendants	relatives
evergreen	plants and trees that do not lose their leaves in winter
industrial revolution	when people move from working by hand on farms to working with machines in factories
industrialized	describes a country which uses machinery in making products and in farming
kami	Shinto spirits which live in sacred places such as rocks, trees, mountains, lakes and rivers
kimono	traditional dress for both men and women, made of silk, with broad sleeves and a sash
prefecture	a state or territory
samurai	warrior soldiers who formed a ruling class until the 1800s
sensei	teacher
shoguns	military rulers who controlled the emperor and ruled Japan for almost 700 years
tatami	thick straw mats which line the floors of traditional Japanese houses
terrace	a flat piece of land cut into the side of a mountain so that crops can be grown there
torii	elaborate red gateways close to many Shinto shrines
typhoon	a severe storm with high winds and heavy rain

Index